The BOOK

of

MONKEYMINDERS™

*Loving Thoughts
to Still the Monkey in Your Mind*

Margaret L. Clay

www.monkeyminders.com

This is the first printing of *The Book of Monkeyminders*.

Although earlier versions of selected Monkeyminders have been published since 1999, this is the first bound compilation of this magnitude of Monkeyminders.

Cover Image entitled, "I AM THAT"
by Margaret L. Clay

Copyright ©2011 Margaret L. Clay. No part of this publication may be reproduced, stored in a retrieval system, or transmitted, in any form or by any means—electronic, mechanical, photocopying, recording, or otherwise—without written permission of the author.

For more copies and information:
Margaret Clay
P. O. 6391
Savannah, GA 31404
info@monkeyminders.com
www.monkeyminders.com
912-376-8496

ISBN 0-9847268-1-0

Table of Contents

INTRODUCTION 1
A NEW DAY 7
A NEW SONG 8
ALL IS WELL 9
AND LO, I AM WITH YOU ALWAYS 10
AND STILL I RISE 11
ANOINTED 12
ARISE 13
AWAKE MY SOUL 14
BABY STEPS 15
BANDIT 16
BEST BELOVED 17
BLESSING 18
BREATH OF LIFE 19
BREATHE ON ME 20
CHOOSING LIFE 21
CHOOSING TRUTH 22
CLUES 23
COME ALONGSIDE 24
COME AWAY 25
COME FIND ME, LOVE 26
COME LET US REASON 27
COME, LIFE! 28
CONTAINED BY LOVE 29
CONTRARY TO APPEARANCES 30
CURIOUS 31

DANCE OF LIFE	32
DANCIN' IN THE WIND	33
DAWNING	34
DILIGENCE	35
DIRECTION	36
DREAM BIG	37
DREAM BIG—AGAIN	38
EDGE	39
EVEN SO	40
FEARLESS FOR LOVE	41
FINDING OUR WAY	42
FINDING YOUR PASSION	43
FOREVER ALWAYS	44
FORGIVEN	45
FREEDOM	46
GETTING READY	47
GOOD-BYE	49
GRACE	50
GRACE IN STILLNESS	51
HACKLES	52
HELP	53
I AM THAT	54
I AM THE ONE	55
I CHOOSE LIFE	56
I CHOOSE LOVE	57
I CHOOSE PEACE	58
IF YOU WANT TO BE HELD	59
IN BETWEEN	60

IN EACH MOMENT	61
IN THE FLOW	62
INTEGRITY	63
JERRY'S PRAYER	64
KEEP MOVING	65
LIVING WITH LOVE	66
LOVE EVERLASTING	67
LOVE IN COLOR	68
LOVE IN HAND	69
LOVERS	70
MISTAKEN IDENTITY	71
MISUNDERSTOOD	72
MORE SHALL BE REVEALED	73
MORE THAN ENOUGH	74
NO WAY!	75
OH JOY!	76
OFTEN, ALWAYS	77
ONCE UPON A PALM	78
ONLY LOVE	79
OPEN DOORS	80
OPENING	81
PARTING WATERS	82
PEACE	83
PEACE NOW AND ALWAYS	84
PEACEFUL SHORES	85
PERCEPTIONS	86
PERFECT AND WHOLE	87
PERMISSION	88

PLEASE AND THANK YOU	89
POWER	90
PRACTICE BEING	91
READY, SET, GO	92
REMEMBER MY LOVE (Mallard)	93
REMEMBER MY LOVE (Mountains)	94
REMEMBER WHO YOU ARE	95
REMEMBER WHO YOU ARE, MY BELOVED	96
REST, BELOVED	97
RISING	98
SEASONS OF LIFE	99
SENSING LIFE	100
SHORTCOMINGS	101
SHOWING UP	102
SO MUCH MORE	103
SOMETHING BIGGER	104
SPEAK NOW	105
SPILLING OVER	106
SPIRIT	107
SPIRIT DANCE	108
SPRING RAIN	109
STAND TALL	110
THE COMPANY WE KEEP	111
THE LORD IS MY SHEPHERD	112
THE STONE IS ROLLED AWAY	113
TOO BUSY	114
TROUBLE	115
TRUE NATURE	116

UPON RISING	117
WAITING FOR SPRING	118
WAITING IN THE WINGS	119
WAKE UP	120
WASH ME	121
WELCOME, BELOVED	122
WELCOME HERE	123
WELCOMING MIRACLES	124
WELLSPRING	125
WHITHER THOU GOEST	126
WHOA, NELLIE!	127
WINDING ROAD	128
WINDING ROAD (Isaiah)	129
WINGS	130
WITH LOVE	131
WORKOUT	132
YES TO LIFE	133
YES!	134
EPILOGUE: MORE LOVING THOUGHTS	135

ACKNOWLEDGEMENTS

ABOUT THE AUTHOR

ALSO BY MARGARET

INTRODUCTION

It feels like a lifetime ago when my dear friend and mentor Pat Peret introduced me to the idea of spiritual dialoguing. She explained it as a way of connecting with the Voice of Truth within myself. Desperately feeling the need for guidance, I began this process which has been one of the single most life-changing practices for me.

At the time, God and I were not on speaking terms. I had become jaded, if not devastated, by the religious language and views surrounding me. I wasn't at all sure I wanted to hear what God might say to me. And I seriously doubted that *if* "He" spoke, I would like what "He" had to say.

Pat suggested that in my journaling I ask a question and wait for the most loving voice I could imagine to answer. Initially, *she* was the most loving voice. She had a habit of saying a few statements over and over. Phrases I'd not heard before. Unsettling, frustrating, and only much later, comforting. Phrases like "All is well;" "more shall be revealed;" "this too shall pass."

In time as I learned to sit in silence with myself, I discovered how to walk myself out of whatever hell I'd created. I discovered not just peace, but a *way* to find peace. More importantly, I discovered that I was not alone. I came to experience God in much more loving, supportive, intimate ways. I learned to find God all over the place, even in the same Judeo-Christian texts that I had found so troubling.

The writings in this book are excerpts from my spiritual dialogues. They were written for my benefit, my comfort, my direction. If anyone else finds value in them, it simply confirms for me the Spirit that connects all of us.

The name *Monkeyminders* came as a shower thought—one of the places for some of my best ideas. The following phrase came in a subsequent shower: *loving thoughts to still the monkey in your mind*. Initially, Monkeyminders took the form of little cards, each with a different message. For over ten years, I have handed them out to friends and strangers. More often than not, the response has been something like, "How did you know? This was just what I needed today!"

I am grateful for the Presence of God in my life and the Voice that speaks to me. I am aware that this Voice is available to all who find the time to be still and listen—*really* listen. This practice has not come naturally to me; thankfully, God is proving to be a patient Presence.

Having come to a belief that the God who spoke to Moses from a burning bush was self-proclaimed beyond name or definition (hence the phrase "I AM THAT I AM"), I have chosen to use more general references for God in attempts to make room for Love in Its Purest Essence with the intention of tripping as few emotional wires as possible—mine or anyone else's. I make no attempt to define or defend anyone else's beliefs. I trust the reader will take what is useful in these pages and leave the rest.

Some of these Monkeyminders are Spirit's message to me; some are my prayers to Spirit. As you read this book, I invite you to enjoy your own conversation with the Divine. My hope in sharing these words is to encourage you to cultivate your inner dialogue and reconnection to your deepest Truth. I have experienced that when I become aware of Truth, it does in fact bring a sense of freedom and clarity.

There is no real order to this book. Because each Monkeyminder is an excerpt from a larger text, I have chosen to list them alphabetically by title. Consider the possibility that "less is best" as you savor these little nuggets. There is no hurry, no real beginning, no end. Imagine the repetition of whatever feels most loving to be as drops of water on a dry sponge. Allow that energy to "satisfy your desire in scorched places" that you might be "like a watered garden, and like a spring of water whose waters do not fail" (Isaiah 58:11).

I have left extra room around each Monkeyminder for you to document your own inspirations and responses. But why stop there? Read, stop, enjoy, savor, listen, record, and know that "Love is always closer than your next breath."

The BOOK

of

MONKEYMINDERS™

*The LORD longs to be gracious to you.
Therefore He waits on high to have compassion on you....
He your Teacher will no longer hide Himself, but your eyes
will behold your Teacher. Your ears will hear a word
behind you, "This is the way, walk in it,"
whenever you turn to the right or to the left.*

Isaiah 30:18-21

A NEW DAY

The success and survival of sailors depend
on their ability not only to do their job
but also to watch and listen
for what else is needed for smooth sailing.
Thus is the paradox of stillness in motion.
Whatever the tide,
this too shall pass and with it,
more shall be revealed with each new day.
And so it is, for all shall be well.

Margaret L. Clay

A NEW SONG

Having risen yet again,
the phoenix with feet extended
dances on its tail feathers
to the beat of a new song.

ALL IS WELL

Come walk with Me today.

Bask in My Love.

Protect your tender heart

from all that feels unloving.

Be gentle today—with yourself.

Do what you have energy for,

but force nothing.

Margaret L. Clay

AND LO, I AM WITH YOU ALWAYS

Remember, that whether you are at home or not,
whether you feel Me or not,
I AM always with you.
I never tire of your company.
I AM never too weak to carry you,
but I do so sparingly
so that your own strength can grow.
You are My child,
in whom I find great delight.

AND STILL I RISE

Smoke not yet cleared,

Feathers still afloat,

A whisper emerges from the ashes:

"And still I rise."

Margaret L. Clay

ANOINTED

It is time now to step into your authenticity.
Take this mantle. Wear it. Feel it. See it.
Every step you take helps to awaken the world.
As you slough off
the weight of your past and choose joy,
the answers will come.
Simply by saying YES
you allow all good things to flow freely to you
and through you.
Treat yourself with respect and tender loving care.

ARISE

Imagine a mermaid caught in a net.
The more she wrestles,
the more entangled she becomes.
One question changes everything:
"What will it take for you to be free?"
In a split second, she stops thrashing,
and like a bullet,
makes a beeline for a target beyond the net.
Leaving the net behind, she rises from the depths
and into the clearer waters,
ever closer to the Light ahead.

AWAKE MY SOUL

The passion of one soul lies dormant
under the earth plates of the heart
still alive even if undetected from a distance.
Until one day an irrevocable Something shifts
waking this passion out of its slumber.
To the surprise of the world and even itself,
molten life bubbles forth
filling the sky with music
and more color than ever before.
Awake my soul and sing!

BABY STEPS

It's okay

that you don't know everything.

Just put one foot

in front of

the other.

Margaret L. Clay

BANDIT

Trust Me.

When all else fails,

follow your nose!

The Book of Monkeyminders

BEST BELOVED

Play life wholeheartedly,

and see who plays with you.

Shoot straight from your heart.

Margaret L. Clay

BLESSING

Lord, if you will, please bless me.
And when I can't yet see the blessing,
remind me that You're
getting me ready to
receive it.

BREATH OF LIFE

My Love, you are whole.
You are complete.
Your heart is full.
Give from your heart.
Receive My Love from
whence I send it.
This is the Breath of Life.

Margaret L. Clay

BREATHE ON ME

Floating on the waters off Little Tybee,
buoyed effortlessly by the salt water,
I bask in the warm stillness
of the August sun above
and in the cool rhythm of the waves underneath.
Muffled sounds of distant boat engines
suggest I am not alone in my revelry.
In this moment, time ceases to exist.
For the first time ever,
I know what it means to be present.

The Book of Monkeyminders

CHOOSING LIFE

I choose my path to Life:

arm in arm

with eyes wide open.

Margaret L. Clay

CHOOSING TRUTH

Life feeling too big today?
You get to choose your perspective,
moment to moment.
In choosing to wake up to Truth,
you see the beauty of the world.
Fall asleep,
and you're prey to nightmares.
You have all you ever need
to be all you want to be.

CLUES

Don't push yourself

onto anyone or into anything.

One step at a time.

Then pause to listen

for your next clue.

Keep dancing.

Life is fluid.

Let it be so.

And so it is.

Margaret L. Clay

COME ALONGSIDE

Together we are called
to move mountains, not by might
but by collective focus and intention.
In this way our light is so intensified
as to be the lighthouse in the darkest storm,
even to ourselves.

COME AWAY

At any moment that is less than peace,
there is the invitation:
"Come away, My Beloved."
Breathing deeply into the "sshh's"
long enough makes room
for the "aahh's" to naturally follow.

Margaret L. Clay

COME FIND ME, LOVE

No longer grasping in the empty air,
No longer fainting from unfulfilled desire,
I now wait quietly in this Sacred Silence,
Profoundly aware of the nearness of Love.

COME LET US REASON

With all the colors of the light spectrum,
and also the colors of the chakras in our bodies,
the fullness of life is present.
So too in community, there are individuals,
with individual colors,
blended together into a radiant collective.

COME, LIFE!

Come, Life, and take me.
Come, Life, and use me.
Let me awaken to what is in this experience
and discover who I really am.

CONTAINED BY LOVE

Resting in the Loving Arms of the Divine,
my soul is restored
in the red glow of Stillness.
As wordless joy bubbles up and spills over,
I move with purpose into the world
and know that all is surely well.

Margaret L. Clay

CONTRARY TO APPEARANCES

In all the unsureness of life,
you can be sure of Me.
All else changes, and yet
you are all forever one with Me
and with each other.
Trust Me in this process.
Remember, My Love,
I AM with you always.

CURIOUS

Dare to be curious

for the fullness of Life and Love

in all its expressions!

Margaret L. Clay

DANCE OF LIFE

We are together a living, breathing body of Spirit.
Let us therefore join in the Dance of Life with the
assurance that just as
inhale follows exhale,
so the flow of giving and receiving
reflects a natural evidence
of being fully alive.

DANCIN' IN THE WIND

There is magic in the air.
It has always been there,
available to anyone
who sits still enough to notice.
There is no need for drama as you discover
how delicious life really is
in its most basic essence.
You are whole.
You are complete.
We are One.

Margaret L. Clay

DAWNING

No matter how dark the night,
the dawn inevitably appears
and brings with it new colors,
new life, new ways of being
until at last the white light of the Divine
dissolves all mysteries,
all questions, all needs
simply with Its Loving Presence.
Surely, Love is always closer
than our next breath,
ever watchful and waiting for us
with deepest compassion.

DILIGENCE

Stay close to Me. Mind your own doorstep.

Be diligent to love and diligent

to surround yourself

with those pursuing Love.

Listen closely to Me.

Sing. Laugh. Dance.

In the song and dance

you become part of the solution.

Leave the problems to Me.

ACT AS IF all is well…for it surely is.

Margaret L. Clay

DIRECTION

Always carry with you a map

that will lead you back home

when you've discovered

that you've

wandered

away.

DREAM BIG

Dream BIG.

Dream in color.

Dream in detail.

Then entrust your dreams to Me.

Margaret L. Clay

DREAM BIG—AGAIN

A splash of color.
Sweeping movements.
A brush perhaps?
And a brown handle to go along?
Paint your dreams with color, variety, distinction.
Dare to go to the far edges of
your highest dreams, and then go even further.
Into the abyss of the unknown,
you may find an even greater expression
of your highest self.

EDGE

So, you are yet again on the edge
of living flat out
and you don't want to fall?
No edge, no flying!

EVEN SO

I love you, Sweetheart.
Dare to BE with Me.
Listen for My Voice.
Don't run away.
Let Me hold you.
You are perfect to Me:
uniquely you, completely comprehensible,
clear, and wonderful.
Let Me be your security.
I gave you your heart's desires, not to tease you,
so that you may experience abundant life.

FEARLESS FOR LOVE

Be present with each moment.
You ARE on your path. All is well.
As you continue to know and verbalize your truth,
and as you continue to allow your underbelly to be
exposed to safe and loving hearts,
you will hear My Word behind you,
and you will step even further on your path.
I have not called you this far to leave you.
There's more. So much more.
Practice no attachments.
Take in; release. Inhale; exhale.
Hold tight; let go.
Know clearly; welcome the mystery.
There is no arrival point on this journey.
Listen carefully at each moment.
Joy is all around you.
THIS is who you are.
THIS is who you came here to be.
Join with Me in celebrating who you really are.
Embrace your Truth and watch time disappear
as you live your seamless life of joy and brilliance.

Margaret L. Clay

FINDING OUR WAY

In the murkiness of life's greatest challenges,
black ink meanders aimlessly across the page.
Once saturated with purposeless blackness,
images start to appear.
An elephant for memories to cherish,
a beloved dog-child now gone,
a woman in mourning.
But there's more.
A hummingbird of hope,
a dove skimming on the water just because it can,
a warm smile of sunshine centerfold,
and a phoenix for transformation.
May we hold the past and the present,
strength forged in the darkness
making true colors even brighter
as we continue finding our way.

FINDING YOUR PASSION

Wherever you find your passion,
there also you will find your leading.
Listen to your own flow
and go with it!

Margaret L. Clay

FOREVER ALWAYS

Give people your Truth.
Held in, it becomes baggage.
Let go, it frees you and everyone else.
Say what you need to say.
Give what you have to give.
Let all be done in love.

FORGIVEN

Washed of all fear,

wrapped in a warm blanket of forgiveness,

held in the Arms of Love

close enough to hear Its Heartbeat

until I remember once again

who I really am.

FREEDOM

Take no prisoners.

None.

Not even yourself.

Let all go free.

Release all with loving kindness.

Give to yourself what you wish from others.

Let all be done in love.

GETTING READY

Get ready for the ride of your life.
Surely it comes just as naturally
as the incoming tides.
My Love for you is uncontainable.
My Heart aches for you to know Me.
Receive My Love; wallow in it; laugh in it;
let it free you to be the incredible,
bright light that you are.
The world needs what you have to give.
No time to waste. Let Me love you.
I have SO much to pour onto you, into you.
You can do all things. ALL THINGS.
I know your heart.
Your prayers have not gone unnoticed.
Get ready for the ride of your life.
This IS the ride of your life.
All things, Love, all things.

Margaret L. Clay

GO GENTLY

Go gently into this world, My Love.
You are finding new strength,
new direction.
Like Lazarus, you have come forth.
I see you strong, grounded, purposeful,
focused, loving and playful,
an integral part of All That Is.
The dance has begun—
the same dance that has always been
and will forever be.
Let the music fill your heart, your lungs,
and be always on your tongue.

The Book of Monkeyminders

GOOD-BYE

Clear good-byes
make room for
clear hellos.

Margaret L. Clay

GRACE

Don't wait for an excuse

to be generous

with yourself

and with others.

GRACE IN STILLNESS

In the tiniest of tinies
there lives a heart
full of grace and stillness,
full of knowing and wonder.
Open to All That Is,
celebrating each moment:
purposeful without agenda
fiercely tender
extravagantly simple.

Margaret L. Clay

HACKLES

See the perfection in all.
When your hackles get raised,
LISTEN for the SILENCE.
As you listen,
you will find Me,
and your wrestling will fade
into loving peace.
Celebrate life
now and always.

The Book of Monkeyminders

HELP

When I realize
only Grace can help me now,
I find that Grace
is all the help I need.

I AM THAT

Whatever your greatest inklings of desire,
I have for you so much more.
Trust Me, and you will not be disappointed.
Expect greatness, grandness, something new.
Let Me surprise you with the impossible!

I AM THE ONE

It's not all up to you.

Let Me love you.

Let My Love in.

Trust Me to provide your needs.

All is surely well.

I CHOOSE LIFE

The Truth I want you to know today
is that your Authentic Power is very good.
It is healing and transformative,
for yourself and others.
The world needs your strength
to remember its own.
The world needs your clarity
to see its own truth.
The world needs your loving embrace
to release all illusions
of isolation and separatism.

I CHOOSE LOVE

No longer waiting,
I embrace the fullness of love
that permeates my cells and flows so effortlessly
as to erase any point of origin.
I now choose to be washed clean
by the tides of deep affection
as I learn to give and receive
the Love that is me.

Margaret L. Clay

I CHOOSE PEACE

What would help you move forward gently,
steadily?
What would be easy for you to do?
Baby steps, Love, baby steps.
This is sacred movement. No hurry.
One tiny, loving step at a time.
All is well.
Trust Me—moment by moment.
Go into laughter, and she will release you.
You ARE moving forward.
You CAN do all things, dear. ALL things.
Listen carefully. No assumptions.
What do you hear calling you?

IF YOU WANT TO BE HELD

You are not alone.
You are loved.
You give much to others.
Open your heart wide,
and let them give to you.
Give what you have to give
from your heart.
Leave the rest to Me.

IN BETWEEN

Despite your anguish,
you are not dying.
This is the In-Between.
Pay attention. Breathe.
The dissonance you feel is helping you to shift
from your comfort to yet
a higher experience of life.

IN EACH MOMENT

Show up in each moment
with as much love and kindness
as you can muster.
Look for love, and you will find it.
Listen for love, and you will hear it.
Let every pore, every cell
open itself to love and be loved.
You are doing this even now.
It may feel to you like
you're living in slow motion,
but this is perfect timing.
Let Me love you.
Let all of Me love all of you.

Margaret L. Clay

IN THE FLOW

Receiving My Love and passing it on
happens as a natural flow when you're connected
to your own truth and are pursuing it.
Go forth. Nothing to fear.
Life need not be anything but joyful
if you so choose.

INTEGRITY

You are My beloved,

in whom I find tremendous delight.

Just as you ask others to trust your integrity,

so I ask the same of you.

Margaret L. Clay

JERRY'S PRAYER

Father, forgive us
for we know not what we do.
Father, forgive me
when I think I have a clue.
In all things, let Thy Will, not mine, be done.

KEEP MOVING

Keep moving.

Follow the path of least resistance.

One step at a time. You can't get it wrong.

Love is in the air. It IS the air you breathe.

Breathe in Love. Breathe in Life.

All of it. Inhale the essence of your own spirit.

You already ARE whole.

You really ARE loved.

More than you could ever hope for

or dream of is just around the corner.

Your only task is to get ready.

LIVING WITH LOVE

Beyond thinking to listening.

Beyond imagining to seeing.

Beyond questioning to being.

Beyond wanting to knowing.

Beyond hurting to healing.

Beyond healing to wholeness.

Beyond learning to living with love.

LOVE EVERLASTING

Be strong, Love.
Be the bold woman you are.
Be who you are
and who you have always been.
Clear, strong, powerful, joyful,
passionate, ecstatic, unconquerable,
and still tender, infinitely kind,
exquisitely gentle, unmistakably vulnerable,
always the student, always the lover.
THIS is who you are.
THIS is who you came here to be.
Join with Me in celebrating
who you really are.
Embrace your Truth and watch
time disappear as you live
your seamless life of joy and brilliance.

Margaret L. Clay

LOVE IN COLOR

You are moving through
tremendous waters here—
into the delight of your own becoming.
Through playful stillness,
you inhabit your own skin
with love and tenderness,
and experience the reality that All is Well.
And so it is.

LOVE IN HAND

Your beloved is your butterfly
as you are his.
Keep your hand open.
Let her light where she will.
Wear your bright colors of passion,
adventure, and clarity.
See where he lights.
Remember that whatever is right for one of you
is ultimately right for both of you.

Margaret L. Clay

LOVERS

Lover of my soul,
Your dreams for me so totally go beyond
anything I could imagine.
I am awestruck, profoundly grateful,
so deeply moved at Your Great Goodness on my
behalf. I love You, and I'm learning to love me
through accepting Your Love.
May all who encounter me today
feel encouraged by Your Love.

MISTAKEN IDENTITY

I am open to letting my oldest beliefs about myself
change. It doesn't have to be hard.
It can be like a new dawning,
like a popcorn kernel ready to pop.
Even in childbirth, the baby doesn't crawl out
but is born by the forces of Life
surrounding it.

MISUNDERSTOOD

Just as you dislike being misunderstood, so too,
I pain over being seen as a God of wrath,
punishment, aloofness, and scarcity.
I AM the God of all Creation,
all that is rich and beautiful.
Choose life, if you dare,
in all of its brilliance.

MORE SHALL BE REVEALED

Everything is unfolding as it should.

Continue forward in all you know to do.

Pursue excellence. More shall be revealed.

Love Me. Love yourself.

All is surely well.

Margaret L. Clay

MORE THAN ENOUGH

Not seeing but still believing.
Not feeling but still hoping.
Trusting that rivers in the desert
and roadways in the wilderness
will become evident once this present fog
lifts with the rising sun.

NO WAY!

You are a bumblebee.
'Tho the world tells you flying
is out of the question,
you fly nonetheless. It's who you are.
And today, My Love, tell Me:
who do you wish to say that you really are?

OH JOY!

Random strokes of colored ink
become a host of arms extended in revelry.
What a joy to be alive
and to belong within the collective celebration of
All That Is.

OFTEN, ALWAYS

Come to Me often and always.
Feel My Arms surrounding you.
I who brought you here will never forsake you.
Rest. Breathe.
Feel the reassurance of My Embrace,
the presence of My Breath,
the joy in My Eyes,
the delight I take in fully recognizing you.
Hear the steady beat of My Heart
as you nestle against Me.
As you breathe in Love,
you will KNOW that all is well.

Margaret L. Clay

ONCE UPON A PALM

All is well, dear one. I AM here.
Feel the warmth of My Breath.
Relax into My Arms.
You are My beloved.
You can do all things, Love. All things.
For now, rest. Here in My Arms.
Allow yourself to bask in My Power.
My Gentleness, My Kindness, My Enduring Love,
My Steady Gaze into your soul.
My Joy at being here with you.
I SEE you.
I have never forgotten you.
Rest with Me often.
Know that all is well.

ONLY LOVE

The birth of your own becoming is at hand.

Be witness to your own delivery.

See where it takes you!

OPEN DOORS

My Love, you are not freed from a situation by
resistance to it, but by cooperation with it.
Do not violate the dictates of the Spirit,
but rather wait until the door opens naturally.

OPENING

Broken.
Broken open.
Broken open by Love.
Broken open to love.
Broken open to be loved.
Broken open to Life.
Broken open.
Open.

Margaret L. Clay

PARTING WATERS

I trust You. You have led me through far more insurmountable things than this present trouble.
Surely You have great plans for me.
You did not bring me this far to watch me crash.
I choose peace over drama.
I choose Your Leading over "obligations."
I choose to experience all my movement with wisdom, love and ease. I know that on some level, all is well.

PEACE

There is enough time and resources
to do that which is YOURS to do.
Peace. Be still.
Be with the Stillness,
and then you will watch time collapse
as healing dissolves all illusions.
Only be still so that you can know.

PEACE NOW AND ALWAYS

If you lose sight of peace,
do what it takes to find it again.
This is a moment-to-moment walk.
If you would follow Me,
you must learn to listen and yield
moment to moment.

PEACEFUL SHORES

Only Grace will take me from my trouble
on this shore
to a place that offers a bigger perspective,
to the shore of Peace where we live in the town of
All-Is-Well.

PERCEPTIONS

In any moment where there is peace,
conflict is impossible. They cannot coexist.
They are your perception.
Choose your perception,
and you will experience your choice.

PERFECT AND WHOLE

My dear one, My Beloved,
come to Me with your
bruised heart and
your cut-up knees.
I see you perfectly,
wholly.
You are complete.
You are loved,
and you are lovable.

PERMISSION

For now, leave all your concerns with Me.
You are responsible for no one today
but yourself. You have all the permission
in the world to take the day off if you choose.
Certainly take the day off
from beating yourself up!
What would be loving today?

PLEASE AND THANK YOU

You have called Me.
I AM at your door.
Let your response be,
"Please come in," and
"Thank You for coming."
Your deepest heart's desires are at your fingertips.
No need to grasp for them;
just receive them as I gently place them
into your hand.

Margaret L. Clay

POWER

When I think that I must choose
either love or power,
I experience a loveless power
or a powerless love.
Yet when I remember
that the root of Real Power is Love,
I find a Powerful Love that knows
no limits.

PRACTICE BEING

You have experienced deep pain in your past,
but who you have been seen as
is not who you are.
So you get to practice BEING who you are,
choosing out of the contrast.
Those who give nothing do so
because they think they have nothing to give.
It's not about you.

Margaret L. Clay

READY, SET, GO

What would you like?
You get to choose. Don't quit.
Don't stop looking. Keep exploring.
You're on the tip of an iceberg.
Dare to adventure further with Me,
and you will not be disappointed.
I long to pour out ALL the treasures
of Heaven before you.

REMEMBER MY LOVE (Mallard)

In the beginning,
there were random strokes of blackness.
Returning to the inky darkness, a heart appeared,
then a strangely dressed mallard duck.
A tiny dancer, then a reposeful
and elegant woman of color,
and the back of a man in plaid wearing a straw hat.
The eyes seemed to be looking back
over the shoulders.
"Why?" I wondered.
Only then did the ominous face appear,
held at bay by the reassurance from a now familiar
Voice: "Remember, My Love,
I AM with you always."

REMEMBER MY LOVE (Mountains)

Remember, that whether you are at home or not,

whether you feel Me or not, I AM always with you.

I never tire of your company.

I AM never too weak to carry you,

but I do so sparingly

so that your own strength can grow.

You are My child,

in whom I find extreme pleasure and delight.

REMEMBER WHO YOU ARE

Listen, My Beloved.
Listen in the Silence.
As you become more quiet,
so much clearer becomes your knowing.
I have so much more for you
than you can imagine.
Sit still and let Me tell you
My Dreams for you.
I long to share their reality with you.
Only be still and you will know.

REMEMBER WHO YOU ARE, MY BELOVED

I enjoy BEING with you.

I love for you to turn to Me and see Me

and receive My Love. I have so much to give you.

You don't have to figure out anything.

When you are ready,

the how-to's will show up.

For now, just look deep into My Eyes,

and when you see the love I hold for you,

you will remember that all is surely well.

For so it is.

REST, BELOVED

Trust Me, Love.
You will not be disappointed.
You are My beloved. Let Me love you.
Choose intimacy with Me and watch
as all of Heaven rejoices in showering you
with more than you ever dreamed possible.
Come away with Me, My Beloved.
Rest in My Arms. Let Me hold you.
Resist nothing. I AM Safe.
You are safe in My Arms.

Margaret L. Clay

RISING

Truly, you were meant to fly.
You learn to fly in the free-fall.
But I AM still your Safety Net.
So, in the air, feel the wind rushing past you,
the unrestrictedness of your body
off the ground. Play in the air.
And if you are aware,
you will know that the air surrounding you
is surely My Breath as a Hovering Kiss.
I take total delight in you, My Beloved.

SEASONS OF LIFE

Honor your own seasons,

your times of needing more rest,

more exercise, more silence,

and know that it is because of that honored time,

your garden will bear healthy,

bountiful crops for many, many years.

SENSING LIFE

Life is a creation in process.

Test the temperature as you would a baby's bath water. Taste it as you do when experimenting with new recipes. Most of all, find ways to be at home with it, with your life.

All of it.

SHORTCOMINGS

Grace asks that I forgive myself

for my shortcomings

as if they weren't there

because to Him...

they aren't.

SHOWING UP

You all need each other to show up for,

to practice life with. Let Me be God.

You just show up—first, for yourself.

The world is not resting on your shoulders.

Answers to all your questions come in the Silence.

SO MUCH MORE

Dare to believe Me for good,
for something beyond anything
you've ever experienced before.

Margaret L. Clay

SOMETHING BIGGER

You have asked Me for specific things,
and I have heard you.
Now put your requests aside, and get ready to give
so that you will be ready to receive.
Let Me create something bigger, brighter for you.
Life is exciting.

SPEAK NOW

It's okay to have feelings.

You can speak for yourself now.

Let Love in.

Breathe in Love.

You give more easily than receive.

Practice receiving.

Don't push away.

Let Love in,

and know that it is safe

to do so.

All is well.

Margaret L. Clay

SPILLING OVER

In receiving all that Love has for us,
we take in nourishment on all levels.
Then finding our cups full,
we can't help but spill over onto each other.
Today, let us accept the Grace that teaches us to
let in love and nourishment.

SPIRIT

Staring at the blank canvas before me,
I am sure there are no pictures in me to paint.
But something moves inside
and prompts first one sweep, then another,
moving through every available color,
covering nearly every available space.
Lost in time, captivated by the process,
I hear a soft song in the distance.
Pausing in my revelry,
I realize the singer is me
and the song is, "Just As I Am."
There I laugh, knowing the meaning at last:
my only calling is to be my most Authentic Self
and to discover Freedom
lying in the expression of this Truth.

Margaret L. Clay

SPIRIT DANCE

This life comes in this form but once.
So laugh! So dance!
So sing! So love!
Live then in ecstasy
and delighted intention.
Be ever ready to choose again.
Always, always listen
for the whisper of the breeze.
And lo, I AM with you always,
even to the end of the age.

SPRING RAIN

Though this ground has long been fallow,
still the rains fall gently on my heart,
misting the cracked earth,
covering it with sweet kisses,
softening its crust, making it possible
for new seedlings to emerge.
Tiny sweet greenness appears,
reaching bravely heavenward,
knowing nothing more than the desire
to experience more life,
the resurrection of a life yet to be lived.

Margaret L. Clay

STAND TALL

Neither hurry nor waiting are needed now.
Beloved, look around:
Your pallet is gone.
You are in fact walking!
Your only job has been to respond
to My Call to stand—
and you have.
Well done, My Child!

THE COMPANY WE KEEP

It's in your nature—

and everyone's—

to be excellent and forgiving.

Look for love,

forgiveness,

excellence in yourself

and in others.

Look for connection,

and you will not be disappointed.

THE LORD IS MY SHEPHERD

STOP!

Stop wrestling.

Just stop. Let go.

No concern for the ticking of the clock.

You have all the time you need

to become all you'd like to be.

For now, be here with Me.

THE STONE IS ROLLED AWAY

There's a quickening I feel.
It's the time of the In-Between.
I can almost feel its edge
where I will meet my next chapter
and be surprised by the new life
yet to experience.

TOO BUSY

Another busy day?
When is a good time to take care of yourself?
What would be loving for you today?

TROUBLE

My Garden is full of color and variety.
Each season brings new flowers
appropriate for its time.
Trust Me with the colors, the timing, the growth.
Only take time to notice what shows up.
Savor it, and open yourself to the next blossom
yet to be revealed.
Take time to receive these truths
into your heart, and you will feel
their transformative power at work in you.

Margaret L. Clay

TRUE NATURE

Everyone everywhere longs to discover
his or her true, full nature.
Let your light, your love
be such a mirror as to reflect
their true nature
back to them.
Start with yourself.

UPON RISING

At the Root of All Things exists a Safe Container.
Once acknowledged,
It provides courage to open wide to Life
and Wisdom to see that only Love prevails
because Love is all there is.
At the sound of the Beloved's Call,
so begins the Dance
where jewels of Authenticity bring us Home
at day's end in harmony with All That Is.

Margaret L. Clay

WAITING FOR SPRING

Know that even during illness,
there is a time of readiness.
Rest as your body requires.
Be still.
This is no detour but a part of the Big Picture.
In regrouping quietly,
you make room for strength ahead.
Depth before breadth.
Hibernation before spring.
Honor the cycles.
Bask in this time of luxurious time.
All is well.

WAITING IN THE WINGS

Waiting in the Quiet is an art like dancing.
Just let your body respond
to the Music Within, to the question:
"What would love do now?"
All is happening in perfect time.

Margaret L. Clay

WAKE UP

There is a cry from the belly of the earth
for the souls who inhabit the earth
to wake up, choose Love, choose Life.
Will you awaken?

WASH ME

First, anointing.
Then a breath of time
before external changes appear.
Patience, Love. I AM here with you.
Remember the washing of your fears,
the warm blanket of forgiveness.
I AM indeed holding you.
Feel the energy of My Love surrounding you.

Margaret L. Clay

WELCOME, BELOVED

Reveal to me my worth in Your Eyes, dear God.
Grant me the courage to embrace
all that I am in You
and all that You are in me.

WELCOME HERE

The strength each of you has found within offers
safety to be vulnerable with each other.
The collective strength can bear any pain.
It's okay to feel, to go forward,
to acknowledge the dark sides and to know
that you need not analyze, fix,
or shoo them away. Let them be.
Sit with them in a loving space,
and watch My Light creep in like the sunrise.
All is surely well.
I love you, My dear one.

Margaret L. Clay

WELCOMING MIRACLES

Father, I surrender my day to You.
I choose to get out of the way of any miracles
You may have in mind for me today.
I have my plans, but I submit them to You.
You have a higher view and may have better ideas.
Thank You for all the details of my life.
I love You, Lord. Clearly,
You want my absolute good.
I surrender my best thoughts to Your Great Plan.

WELLSPRING

Stay open to Love,

wherever it shows up.

Remember from Whence it comes,

and return there constantly.

I AM the wellspring for your heart,

your lifeline.

Margaret L. Clay

WHITHER THOU GOEST

Over the hills and through deep waters
travel the feet of undying devotion.
Faithfulness in listening to God's whispers
at each step ensures an ancient path
full of surprises.

WHOA, NELLIE!

Find what fills you up today and bask in it.
Only stop here awhile with Me first.
Stop here in the place that is full, abundant,
prosperous, generous, and light.
Stop here awhile,
and only then choose your day
from the quiet place.
Answers will come when you need them.

Margaret L. Clay

WINDING ROAD

Be present now

…and now

…and now.

Stay.

Stay present.

Speak from THAT place,

the QUIET PLACE.

It will be loving.

Slow to speak,

slow to anger,

slow to react.

Listen. *Listen.*

Listen to Me.

Listen to others.

Hear what they aren't saying.

WINDING ROAD (Isaiah)

"Do not call to mind the former things,
or ponder things of the past.
Behold, I will do something new.
Now it will spring forth.
I will even make a roadway in the wilderness,
rivers in the desert."

Isaiah 43:18-19

Margaret L. Clay

WINGS

You are My bumblebee,

and I AM your wings.

WITH LOVE

I love you, Sweetheart. I cherish you.
You are My baby girl.
I celebrate who you are
and all you bring to Me and to this world.
There is no one in the world like you:
so strong, so gentle, so creative,
so powerful, so vulnerable.
Feel My Loving Embrace, My Bosomy Hug.
Let Me hold you close and kiss your face.
Now, let Me look at you.
Yes, you ARE beautiful.
As I look into your eyes,
I see all the way to your soul
and recognize the familiarity that meets My Eyes.
I see you.
I love you. I honor you.
I recognize you. I appreciate you.
I celebrate you.
Even in this, I AM with you always.

WORKOUT

Trust Me with the practical working out
of your beliefs. Trust Me with your success,
your peace, your contentment,
your prosperity, your dreams.

YES TO LIFE

I am open to learn what I need to learn,

hear what I need to hear,

see what I need to see,

love how You would have me love.

I embrace clear boundaries

and release all obstacles to a full, loving,

healthy, balanced life.

Margaret L. Clay

YES!

I am open to receiving
the fullness of Life
You have for me.

EPILOGUE: MORE LOVING THOUGHTS

The world is in great need of loving kindness, individually and collectively, in order to heal and move forward. May you be inspired. May you be comforted by the One who is always with you and for your Highest Good. May you find your way back to peace when you've lost it. May you relish the clarity that comes from sitting in the Silence. May you choose the path of Love as you understand it.

Despite any illusions to the contrary,
you are always and forever
God's beloved.

If you don't believe it,
just ask and listen
for the Response.

All is well,
And all is well.
And all is *still* well.

May all be blessed by the lives we live.

ACKNOWLEDGEMENTS

Over 25 years ago in a former life, my wise friend Al Panu shared with me a passage from the Old Testament (Isaiah 30:15-21). The words felt important and foreign. I put them to music so that I would remember them until such time as their mystery would reveal itself to me. It took another 12 years before I experienced the comfort in "hearing a word behind me, 'This is the way, walk in it.'" This promise sustained me during my years of "dark night" and continues to encourage me daily. A piece of this passage is the inscription in the front of this book.

Pat Peret, as mentioned in my introduction, taught me the practice of spiritual dialogue which is the foundation for the body of this book. She also introduced me to the Observer Within that has enabled me to view my circumstances objectively and therefore make more conscious choices instead of react or recoil. Through her mantras such as "all is well," I learned that simple repetition with kindness is often the best teacher. She introduced me to an art form that I have come to know as "intuitive painting." The cover design was painted using this technique. More shall be revealed about this work in my next book.

I am grateful for everyone and everything that has reinforced the presence of a living, loving God who is actively engaged in my life. Letting me read the "red letters" of Jesus in the New Testament as a child, my mother, Anita Clay, first introduced me to the paradox of a holy and personal God. My father, Thomas Clay, taught me to memorize pieces of the Episcopal prayer book as I sat on his lap before going off to bed. His faith was as private as it was unwavering. My brother, Henry, has been a beacon of God's tenderness in the humility of his own spiritual journey and in his faithful belief in me.

Linda Ellis and Jeannie Galindo may have been the first people who saw in me what was beyond the mirror. Debbie Goodwin was the first to encourage me to write a book. My wonderful friend of 33 years, Carol Kahn, has encouraged me to find my voice, my strength, and my way. Thank you to the healing communities of Unity of Savannah and Asbury Memorial United Methodist Church. Friends who have encouraged me to write, strangers who have experienced the power of Monkeyminders in a passing exchange, those who have believed in me even if they could not continue on the same path with me—individually and collectively—all have supported me in more ways than I express. Please know that each of you has made a huge difference in my life, and I would not be here if not for your loving participation in my life. In truth, Monkeyminders seem to have a life of their own, and it feels more like my "charge" to care for them and make them available to a larger audience.

It has taken the practical help of Kate Greene, Carol Kahn, and Pat Andres to pull this book together. Their computer expertise and editorial eyes have made a world of difference in this finished product.

Special thanks to Gerard Patrick Dunn, close friend, business guide and spiritual cheerleader. "Jerry's Prayer" belongs to him. With his passing this summer, I am left with the echoes of his impassioned encouragement to help me navigate new waters. So many that have left my life in one way or another still reside in my heart and continue to offer their wisdom in the Silence where we are reunited in Spirit.

And lo, I AM with you always,
even to the end of the age.

Matthew 28:20

ABOUT THE AUTHOR

Born into a Southern Episcopal family, Margaret's spiritual journey began early and has been at least as circuitous as those Israelites who took 40 years to cover a 2-week trek on their way to the Promised Land. Along the way, her teachers have come from the heart of Christ, the mindfulness of the Buddha, the Upanishads of the Hindus, and the wisdom of the Sufis. More than anywhere else, her spiritual foundation is based on her personal experience with the Divine through the practice of cultivating Stillness and the loving presence of others actively pursuing their Truth.

Margaret holds a BSHE in Child Development from the University of Georgia in Athens, GA, and an MA in Curriculum and Instruction from the University of Colorado in Colorado Springs, CO. She is certified as a Life Coach through Success Unlimited Network® and is pursuing a Master Certified Coach certification through the International Coaching Federation. Her sincere intention is to savor each moment, foster safe and loving relationships (with oneself, the Divine, and others), and inspire others to cultivate their innate brilliance and wisdom. She currently lives in Savannah, GA, with two of her greatest teachers and companions, Sophie and Pierre.

ALSO BY MARGARET

Books
It is Time. A hardback, full-color gift book, written and illustrated by Margaret.

(Coming Soon) A bound collection of Monkeyminders and original artwork.

Other Creations:
Monkeyminders: Dream Big Collection. A set of 21 business-card size Monkeyminders, each illustrated with original paintings by Margaret.

Original paintings and prints by Margaret.

Silk scarves. Hand painted by Margaret, each with their own Monkeyminder.

> For more copies and information:
> Margaret Clay
> P. O. Bo 6391
> Savannah, GA 31404
> 912-376-8496
> info@monkeyminders.com
> www.monkeyminders.com

www.ingramcontent.com/pod-product-compliance
Lightning Source LLC
Chambersburg PA
CBHW051804040426
42446CB00007B/505